Contents

Great southern land

Much warmer than Britain and ten times as large …

British song, 1786

We are all Australians with different backgrounds and different family histories. Some people are **descendants** of the first Australians – the Aboriginal and Torres Strait Islander Peoples. Some people were born in another country and came to live in Australia. Others were born in Australia but have family members, or **ancestors**, who came to Australia from other countries. They came to Australia to start a new life.

Aboriginal and Torres Strait Islander Peoples have lived in Australia, for more than 50 000 years. In 1787, hundreds of people, were sent from England to Australia – the 'great southern land'. These people were mainly **convicts** and their guards. They were sent because the prisons in England had become too full and also because the English government wanted to begin a settlement in Australia.

This was a difficult time for both the Aboriginal people and the new European settlers. It was the meeting of two vastly different worlds. It was also the beginning of a new chapter in the history of our amazing country, Australia.

Did you know?
A town in Queensland is called 1770 after the year that Captain James Cook landed there.

descendants people related to a person born before them
ancestors people related to a person and born after them
convicts people found guilty of a crime

In general the Convicts have behaved well, I saw them all yesterday for the first time they are quiet and contented. Tho' there are among them some compleat villains.

First Fleet Convicts

This painting shows a group of First Fleet convicts about to depart England for Australia.

LET'S FIND OUT

- Why were convicts sent to Australia?
- How did the convicts get to Australia?
- Where was the first British settlement built?
- What was life like for the convicts?
- How did the arrival of the British affect the Aboriginal people?

The First Fleet

On the 13 May 1787, a fleet of 11 ships set sail from England bound for Australia.

These ships became known as the First Fleet. They carried almost 1500 passengers. Around 775 of them were prisoners known as convicts. The rest of the people on board included naval officers and crew, marines, officials, women and children.

A map showing the route taken by the First Fleet, from England to Australia.

The idea

Life was very difficult in England in the 1700s. Jobs were hard to find, and some people had to steal food to feed their families. There was lots of crime, and the prisons were overcrowded. The British government reduced the number of convicts in the prisons by sending some to Australia.

Getting ready

Captain Arthur Phillip was put in charge of the First Fleet and the **expedition**. He was responsible for its safe arrival. He also had to set up the new **colony** once the fleet arrived.

The fleet needed to take many supplies with them, as the land where they were settling had no shops, no roads, no crops and no factories.

Captain Arthur Phillip

Supplies aboard the First Fleet

animals	one bull, 87 chickens, 35 ducks, two horses, 19 goats, kittens, puppies
furniture	one piano, beds, hammocks, tents
food	rice, flour, oats, butter, brandy, sugar, cocoa, coffee, spices, raisins, beef, pork, water
tools	hammers, fishing lines, saws, scissors, axes, spades, wheelbarrows
plants	apple, banana, lemon, orange, strawberry, sugar cane, Spanish reed, cotton, various seeds
transport	six carts, four timber carriages
other	books, candlesticks, saucepans, plates, bowls

expedition a journey to get something in particular done
colony land on which people from another country settle

The journey

The journey from England to Australia was long and difficult. The First Fleet faced bad weather and rough seas.

The convicts lived in cramped, crowded conditions. Some were chained and behind bars. They spent day after day underneath the main deck. Food was **rationed** and many convicts got sick because of the filthy conditions. It is thought that 48 people died on the journey to Australia.

The convicts lived on the prison deck, below the main deck.

The arrival

After a long and dangerous journey the 11 ships arrived safely on the shores of Port Jackson, New South Wales. The journey took eight months and one week.

On 26 January 1788, Captain Phillip set foot on land and raised the British flag. This was the beginning of European settlement in Australia.

Captain Phillip raising the British flag

rationed shared out in a fixed amount

Breakaway task

Remembering

1 Write two facts about Captain Arthur Phillip.

2 List 10 items that were taken on The First Fleet's journey.

3 List the important dates from the text. What happened on each of these days?

Understanding

4 Describe the convicts' living areas.

5 Describe how you think the convicts felt being sent to Australia.

Applying

6 Imagine you are Captain Arthur Phillip. Write a letter to the British government telling them about the journey and arrival in Australia.

7 Re-enact the raising of the British flag by Captain Phillip on Australian soil. What would he have said? How would he have felt?

Analysing

8 What are the arguments *for* and *against* sending convicts to Australia? List three points for each side on a T-chart.

Evaluating

9 Suggest five ways to improve the convicts' living conditions on board the ships using pictures and writing.

Creating

10 Write and perform a rap about convicts being transported to Australia.

Living in two worlds

When the British settlers arrived, Aboriginal people were curious yet wary of them. The settlers didn't speak the Aboriginal people's languages, and they had different customs.

William Buckley

Captain Phillip had orders to be friendly to the Indigenous people. But when land was cleared for farming and food hard to find, fighting broke out. People on both sides died.

However, there were many examples of Aboriginal people helping the settlers. One of these is the story of a man called William Buckley. This is one version of what may have happened...

In 1802 in England, William Buckley was caught with a roll of stolen cloth. He was found guilty of stealing and was **transported** to Australia on a convict ship. In the new settlement, he worked long hours in harsh conditions. By the end of 1803, he decided to escape.

curious wanting to learn more about
wary to be careful
customs traditional ways of doing things
transported taken from one place to another

William escaped at night and ran into the bush. He didn't stop until he was far from the convict settlement. Even though he was free, he now faced different problems. What would he eat? Where would he sleep? What would the local Aboriginal people do to him if they found him?

William found berries and shellfish to eat, but he struggled to find enough to survive. As the weeks went by, he became weaker. He was slowly starving to death.

One day, as William staggered through the bush, he noticed a spear in the ground. He grabbed it and used it to help him walk. He walked a little further into the bush and then he fell over.

Two women from the Wathaurong tribe found William on the ground and shook him awake. William was frightened when he saw them staring down at him. The women thought he was the spirit of a dead leader because he had the dead man's spear. They gave him food and water.

The Wathaurong people treated William with kindness. They taught him their language and customs, and how to hunt and gather food. William became a part of their group and stayed with them for 32 years!

As part of the Wathaurong tribe, William dressed in animals skins.

This painting shows William Buckley's escape from the convict settlement.

One day, William came across a small group of British men camped on the beach. He decided to go with these men to see the **governor**. The governor gave William a **pardon**. This meant that he was now a free man!

William then worked as an **interpreter** between the British and the Aboriginal people. But he found this very difficult. He felt that he was never fully part of either group, and that no one trusted him. Two years later he moved to Tasmania. He lived there until his death in 1856.

governor the official in charge of the settlement
pardon excused from past deeds
interpreter someone who can explain what one language means in another language

Breakaway task

Remembering

1 Why was William sent to Australia?
2 Who did the Wathaurong people think William was? Why?

Understanding

3 What part of William's story did you like the most? Why? Create a cartoon strip showing this part of the story.
4 Draw a Venn diagram comparing William's life as a convict to his life as a member of the Wathaurong people.
5 Explain why William didn't enjoy his work as an interpreter?

Applying

6 Find out how the Wathaurong people lived before European settlement. Present your facts on a concept map.
7 Create a digital slide-show about the main events in William's life.

Analysing

8 Do you think the saying, 'You've got Buckley's chance', came from William Buckley's story? Why or why not?

Evaluating

9 Rate William's life on a line graph. Put main events on the horizontal axis and rate them from 0 to 5 on the vertical axis. (0 = very bad; 5 = very good.)

Creating

10 Write an article about finding William Buckley after 32 years. Include a headline, photos, captions and quotes.

Wanted!

Most convicts worked hard building things such as roads and bridges for the settlements. If they disobeyed the officers, they were whipped or even hanged. Some convicts escaped and the government would offer a reward for their capture.

WANTED

MARY McCOY

£20 Reward

Convict Mary McCoy has escaped. His Excellency, the governor, has offered a twenty pound reward to any person who captures Mary McCoy. If a convict captures her, he shall also receive a conditional pardon.

Description: 28 years old. 5 feet 3 inches tall. Slim build. Brown hair, brown eyes. Large scar on the back of left hand.

conditional pardon the freeing of a convict as long as they stayed in Australia

Breakaway task

Remembering

1 How much money was offered for Mary's capture?
2 Write three facts about Mary McCoy.

Understanding

3 Why do you think Mary escaped?
4 Why might the governor have offered such a high reward for Mary's capture?

Applying

5 Draw the place you imagine Mary might have gone to after escaping. Label your picture.

Analysing

6 Do you think offering a reward would help to capture Mary? Give three reasons to support your answer.
7 Write five questions you would like to ask Mary.

Evaluating

8 How effective is the 'Wanted' poster on a scale of 1 to 10. (10 being the most, 0 being the least.) Explain your rating. What extra information would you include?

Creating

9 Create your own 'Wanted' poster about an escaped convict.
10 Write a script for a television 'news flash' about the escape and capture of Mary McCoy.

We are one

I am Australian is a popular song that celebrates the **diversity** of the Australian people.

I am Australian

Lyrics by Bruce Woodley and Dobe Newton, 1987
Music by Bruce Woodley

Verse 1

I came from the **dreamtime**, *from the dusty red soil plains*
I am the **ancient** *heart, the keeper of the flame.*
I stood upon the rocky shore, I watched the tall ships come.
For forty thousand years I've been the first Australian.

Chorus

We are one, but we are many
And from all the lands on earth we come.
We share a dream and sing with one voice:
I am, you are, we are Australian.

Verse 2

I came upon the prison ship, bowed down by iron chains.
I cleared the land, endured **the lash** *and waited for the rains.*
I'm a settler, I'm a farmer's wife on a dry and barren run
A convict then a free man, I became Australian.

diversity difference
dreamtime when the world was created according to Aboriginal beliefs
ancient very old
the lash a whip guards used to punish convicts

Breakaway tasks

Remembering

1 Who wrote the lyrics to *I am Australian*?

2 According to the lyrics, how many years have the first Australians lived in Australia?

Understanding

3 Who is each verse about? Draw these people and list key words from the song around them.

4 Create a dance to go with the song – use actions to show the meaning of the lyrics.

Applying

5 Find and list other songs or poems about Australia. Choose one to share with your classmates.

6 Create a profile about one of the songwriters. Include interesting facts and illustrations.

Analysing

7 *I am Australian* mentions things that represent Australia. Use these ideas, and some of your own, to create a concept map that represents Australia.

8 Write another verse for the song explaining what makes you Australian.

Evaluating

9 What do you think is the purpose of the song?

Creating

10 Design a CD cover for this song. Make sure your CD cover matches the song's meaning.

Strands in action

Core tasks

1 Make a documentary about a convict coming to Australia on the First Fleet. Create a profile of the convict, and write a script about his or her life in Australia. Use your script, and props, to film your documentary.

2 Plan a radio show about the arrival of the First Fleet in Australia. Include stories and interviews with Captain Cook, convicts and the Aboriginal people. Finish your radio show with a jingle.

Extra tasks

1 Write a 'Did You Know?' fact box about the First Fleet.

2 Write an acrostic poem about Australian convicts.

3 Create a digital slide-show about why people came to Australia.

4 Create a poster about your family history. Include photos, quotes, interviews and stories.

When writing descriptions of places, people, things, and feelings, use interesting adjectives to provide more detail. For example, if someone is happy, are they glad, pleased, cheerful or delighted? These descriptive words provide a clearer picture for the reader. Often a thesaurus can be used as a tool to find descriptive words.